To

From

First published in 1994 by Michael O'Mara Books Ltd
9 Lion Yard, Tremadoc Road, London SW4 7NQ

A CIP catalogue record for this book is available
from the British Library

ISBN 1-85479-967-3

Cover and inside illustrations by Patti Pearce
Design by Mick Keates

Printed and bond in Slovenia by Printing House
Mariborski Tisk by arrangement with Korotan
Italiana

FOR MOTHER

Michael O'Mara Books Limited

A mother is

Always there to turn to for advice -
                        gently given
Always there to understand
Always there to catch me if I fall
Always ready to take my side
Always my strong support in times
                        of trouble

and in return
Always you have my love

A lifetime with you is too short
A gift that cannot be bought
Your love is my treasure
My love beyond measure
Is all I dare offer, unsought.

To give and not to count the cost,
To trust though trust be oft
                betrayed,
To hope where hope is all but lost,
To strive and not to be afraid,
To ask but not to ask in greed,
To offer help to those in need.

You taught me all of this
and blessed me with a mother's kiss

Please be there today, mother,
As you were yesterday.
I need you always.

For you are in my heart, mother,
As you were yesterday
and shall be always.

Parting shall ever grieve
Though even when she leaves
for a world away
in my heart she stays
Her circling arms my shield.

Parting shall ever grieve
Though yet she shall believe
dearest mother
how I love her
These words I beg her read.

When I rise up in the morning
I offer you, mother, my love.
When I go out in the rushing world
my calm is the mother I love.
When I come home in the evening
I love you almost like breathing.
And now day's taken leave of the sun
and the long day is finally done,
I do what I did at day's dawning
and offer you, mother, my love.

Mother, you have given me peace
and the courage to travel the road.
My way is paved with happy days
and my loving shall never cease.
To you, mother is ever owed
love and honour, love and praise.

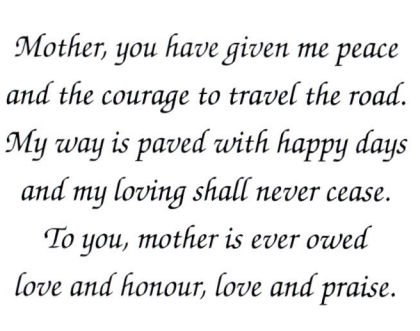

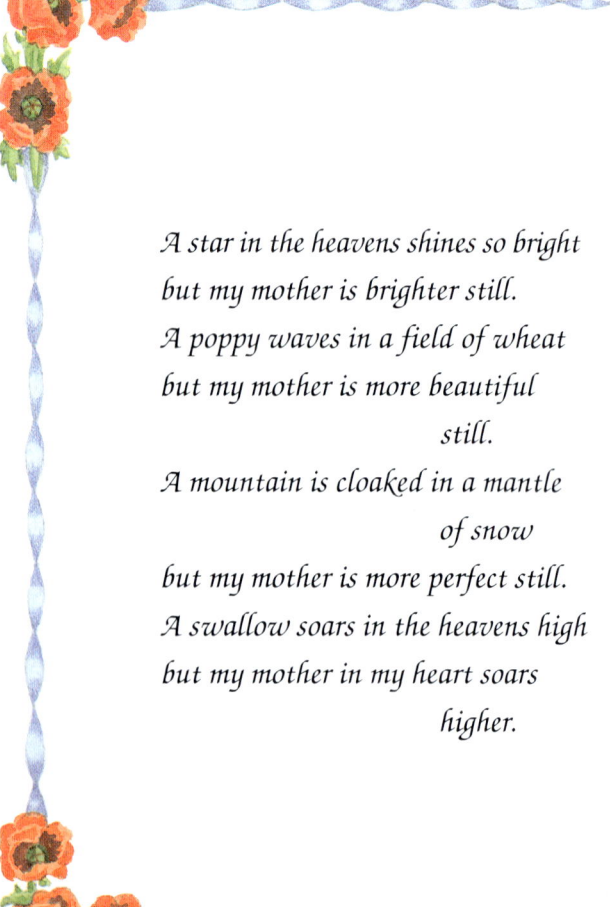

A star in the heavens shines so bright
but my mother is brighter still.
A poppy waves in a field of wheat
but my mother is more beautiful
                              still.
A mountain is cloaked in a mantle
                    of snow
but my mother is more perfect still.
A swallow soars in the heavens high
but my mother in my heart soars
                    higher.

When I was a child, my mother's arms
kept me safe from the world's harms

When I went to school she taught
me this:
that love is learnt from a mother's kiss

When I left home my mother sighed,
for the pain of the parting she could
not hide

Now I'm grown up and my mother's
arms
still keep me safe from the world's
harms.

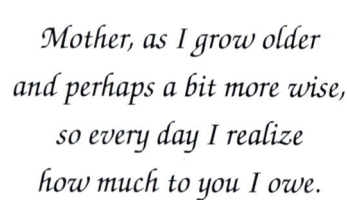

Mother, as I grow older
and perhaps a bit more wise,
so every day I realize
how much to you I owe.

I have been blessed, my mother,
in sharing my life with you.
You are my guiding star, no other
love would do.

Mother puts out her hand
to raise me if I fall.
Mother always understands
when I dare not open the door.
Mother will not desert me
when my way I cannot see
and the flame burns low
or I want to say 'no',
Mother puts out her hand.

It is hard to find words
to say 'thank you'
to the mother loved best in the world
All I can do is to bless you
for knowing I love you, untold.